# ESTHER

*A month in the presence
of the Jewish Queen*

LINDA
OTTEWELL

# kevin
# mayhew

First published in Great Britain in 2019 by Kevin Mayhew Ltd
Buxhall, Stowmarket, Suffolk IP14 3BW
Tel: +44 (0) 1449 737978 Fax: +44 (0) 1449 737834
E-mail: info@kevinmayhew.com

## www.kevinmayhew.com

9 8 7 6 5 4 3 2 1 0

ISBN 978 1 84867 975 7
Catalogue No. 1501597

Cover design by Rob Mortonson
© Image used under licence from Shutterstock Inc.
Typeset by Angela Selfe

Printed and bound in Great Britain

# Contents

# About the Author

Based in Suffolk, Linda has an academic background in modern languages and taught English as a Foreign Language before joining Kevin Mayhew Ltd in 2000 as a proofreader and editor of books and music.

Outside work, Linda is a long-standing member of her local parish church, where she plays the clarinet in the music group, is part of the prayer ministry team and regularly writes and leads intercessions in the Sunday morning services.

Afflicted with an incurable love of studying, in recent years Linda has completed theology and vocation courses by distance learning from St John's Theological College in Nottingham, and a certificate in counselling skills for pastoral care.

Music, reading and handicrafts are firm hobbies, while she can bore for England on the joys of keeping house rabbits and the benefits of Pilates as a means of exercise and relaxation!

Creative writing has been an enduring pastime and Linda is delighted to have prepared and presented her own work for publication, after many years of reading and correcting other authors' proofs.

# Introduction

I wonder what you already know about Esther and why an Old Testament book bears her name? Who was she and when and where did she live? What did she achieve that is so memorable and exactly what is the Book of Esther about? People I've spoken to don't seem to know much beyond the fact that, in the original version, God is never mentioned by name, and that this is one of only two books in the entire Bible named after a woman, the other being Ruth.

My aim has been to look at why Esther and her story are relevant and important today. To what extent can we identify with Esther and what can we learn from her story? At this point, you may be wondering what on earth Christians can discover about God and our walk with him from a book where God *appears* to be absent. It's crucial to hold on to what the Bible teaches us:

> All Scripture is inspired by God and is useful for teaching, for reproof, for correction, and for training in righteousness.
>
> (2 Timothy 3:16)

Remember that Paul was mainly referring to the Old Testament, since not all the New Testament books had been written at that time. God can speak to us today through the most unlikely parts of his Word, even chapters and verses that we might be inclined to dismiss as quite boring. I recently heard about a suicidal prisoner who felt God was telling him to open the copy of the New Testament that had been gathering dust in his cell. This prisoner had a life-changing conversion experience after reading the lengthy genealogy at the start of Matthew's Gospel!

The Book of Esther is short – only 10 chapters – and is the last of the historical books, tucked in between Nehemiah and Job, although the events took place some 30 years before those recorded in Nehemiah. We don't know who wrote Esther – possible contenders are Ezra, Nehemiah or even Mordecai, who is a major player in the story. What seems clear is that the author was a Jew, as evidenced by the Jewish nationalism throughout and the emphasis on the origins of the Jewish Feast of Purim, which is still celebrated by Jews today.

Esther has all the ingredients necessary for a good story and you might want to read it all the way through first, before beginning these devotions. The story is exciting, gripping, inspiring, full of drama and romance, intrigue and subterfuge, conflict, tension and danger. In short, it's a ripping yarn, with a happy ending where evil is overcome, the 'goodies' win and the 'baddies' get their comeuppance. You can imagine an audience cheering and booing the characters accordingly, as in the best of Christmas pantomimes.

However, the Book of Esther is much more than simply a good story. Even though God is not spoken of explicitly, the chapters clearly demonstrate his faithfulness, sovereignty, compassion, grace and mercy and his loving care for his people. God's presence is felt throughout, as, all-powerful and in absolute control of the destiny of his chosen people, he works out his promises, plans and purposes for them and rescues them from the very real danger of total annihilation.

# 1

# Setting the scene

The Book of Esther begins not, as you might expect, with Esther herself, but with Xerxes the Great (known also in some Bible versions as Ahasuerus), ruler of the vast Medo-Persian Empire, which stretched from India in the east to Egypt in the west and included the provinces of Media and Persia and the former empires of Assyria and Babylon.

*Read Chapter 1:1.*

The year is 483BC and most of the story takes place in King Xerxes' palace in Susa, the Persian capital city, 150 miles east of Babylon. Xerxes reigned from 486 to 465BC and he was the son of Darius the First and Atossa, the daughter of Cyrus the First. About 100 years prior to this story's events, King Nebuchadnezzar of Babylon had taken the Jews into captivity and then about 50 years before, Zerubbabel had led the first group of exiles back to Jerusalem following the decree by Cyrus, the

Persian king, permitting them to return. However, many of the Jewish exiles chose to remain in Persia, where they enjoyed great freedom, including the permission to run their own businesses and hold positions in government.

So, something of a history lesson to set the scene, and patience is required to wait a while before Esther even appears, but the background is vital to an understanding of the circumstances of the story and the events faced by Esther and her people.

## Prayer

Heavenly Father, as I begin this study into the life of Esther, may my heart and mind be open to all you want to teach me over the coming days. Help me to understand your Word, take it to my heart and learn from it.

# Xerxes, an absolute monarch

From these opening verses of the first chapter, we learn about the vast extent of King Xerxes' kingdom and the absolute power he exercises over his subjects. The banquet he throws for foreign leaders and his own nobles and officials is meant as a blatant demonstration and display of his power and authority, and a warning to others.

*Read Chapter 1:1-3.*

Consider the standing of King Xerxes, his great power, prestige and sphere of influence. A reading of the Old Testament, and history in general, shows how empires and their rulers rise to great prominence for a time. They have their day but, as with the Babylonians and Assyrians, these empires tumble and fall, only to be replaced by new powers. Xerxes himself met a grisly end when he was murdered in Susa by the captain of his guards, and the Persian Empire eventually fell to Greece.

Think about those leaders of nations in your own lifetime that have seemed invincible yet are no more. In recent years we have seen, amongst others, the downfall of Saddam Hussein in Iraq, and the Libyan leader Colonel Gaddafi. A few years earlier, the Romanian dictator, Nicolae Ceausescu, was deposed and executed, and before that we witnessed the end of the Soviet Union and the reunification of Germany. In 2017, Robert Mugabe finally lost his grip on power in Zimbabwe after many years of autocratic rule.

## Prayer

Lord God, I look to you, the King of kings and Lord of lords. Earthly kingdoms may appear to be all-powerful but one day all nations and their rulers will bow the knee to you and will acknowledge you as Lord. Help me to live in expectation of that marvellous time when Jesus will return to this earth and will usher in your eternal kingdom.

# Earthly treasures

There is no sign of Esther in the story yet; instead even more detail about Xerxes and the opulence of his kingdom.

*Read Chapter 1:4-8.*

Have you ever been on a tour of a splendid royal palace or a sprawling stately home and gardens and stood in awe of how the other half lives? In the world's eyes, Xerxes had it all – power, and wealth beyond most people's wildest dreams. Yet in the final analysis, no amount of wealth could ever stop Xerxes going the way of all human beings: death being the great leveller. All the treasure in the world could have no value for him then. As people are sometimes fond of saying, shrouds have no pockets.

To what extent are people in today's world judged by their material success? Materialism is so inbuilt into our consumer society that we may not even notice its influence on us. Some people search for happiness and contentment in material wealth, acquiring 'stuff', hoping it will satisfy and fulfil their lives. God looks beyond outward appearances of success to the heart. He isn't impressed by wealth and status. In his Sermon on the Mount, Jesus warned against storing up treasures on earth, which may glitter for a while but are only ever temporary. Instead, Jesus told his followers to store up lasting treasure in heaven (Matthew 6:19-21). Where does your treasure lie?

## Prayer

Father God, you call us to live *in* this world but to be different, not *of* the world. May I love you wholeheartedly and be generous with my possessions. Help me to see the difference between what I might desire and what I truly need, for I know that whatever I treasure the most, where my heart is, will determine how I live.

4

# A challenge to the king's authority

Into the story comes not Esther (still more patience is required) but Queen Vashti, sealing her fate by her stubbornness and defiance.

*Read Chapter 1:9-22.*

On the seventh day of the banquet, King Xerxes, used to being obeyed and having his own way, summons Queen Vashti into his presence, so that he can show off her beauty to his guests. When Vashti disregards his authority, doesn't submit to his order and refuses to attend, the king quickly agrees to depose her. Blazing with anger as he is, the king is easily swayed by his experts and their determination that women should respect their husbands and the man should always be head of his household.

Does this seem a totally outdated notion to you in today's world? We need to remember the position of women in society at that time and read the Old Testament in that light. However, following recent complaints about the persistence of inequality in the workplace in England, can we claim that women have achieved the same status as men in our society? Of course, in many countries there still exists a very real oppression of women. In 2012, Malala Yousafzai was shot by the Pakistani Taliban as a punishment for calling for better education for women in Pakistan. Fortunately, she made a full recovery and eventually went on to study at Oxford University. Malala has become a symbol worldwide of the struggle against the oppression of women and in 2014 she was the youngest person ever to win the Nobel Peace Prize.

## Prayer

All people are equal in your sight, Lord, for we are all one in Christ Jesus. Help me to play my part in the fight against oppression, inequality and injustice, however small and insignificant my influence may seem.

# 5

# The search for a new queen

Four years have passed between chapters one and two of the story, during which the king was busy waging war against Greece. Xerxes now remembers Vashti; his anger towards her has been forgotten but he is still advised to find a new queen. In keeping with the grandeur of the kingdom, expensive and elaborate plans are set in motion to replace Vashti.

*Read Chapter 2:1-4.*

So, the search is on for a beautiful new queen and many candidates are rounded up and find themselves part of the king's harem. These girls would have had no choice in the matter, and in the life and culture of the time such behaviour was not even questioned. By modern standards, however, the incident looks like human trafficking and we can only wonder what eventually happened to all these girls. Were they allowed to go back to their former lives once a new queen had been selected or were they destined to remain in the harem?

Human trafficking, a modern form of slavery, is the trade of people in their own country or abroad for forced labour, sexual slavery or commercial sexual exploitation. It's a serious crime and a violation of human rights, and on the increase. Consider stories you have heard about human trafficking and think about the life-changing impact on the individuals concerned.

## Prayer

Lord God, I pray for all those caught up in the misery of human trafficking and forced labour, both in this country and overseas. As a greater awareness of these crimes against humanity grows, may governments and individuals alike begin to take more of a stand.

# Enter Esther into the story

At last the principal character in the story makes her entrance and we begin to suspect what is to come once we read that Esther, likely to be no older than 14 or 15, is 'fair and beautiful'.

*Read Chapter 2:5-7.*

Firstly, we are introduced to Mordecai, a Jew whose forebears had been taken into exile by Nebuchadnezzar, King of Babylon. Mordecai was probably born in Susa and we later learn of his high position in the civil service of the empire that gives him access to the 'king's gate' (Esther 2:19). He has an orphaned younger cousin, Esther, for whom he has taken responsibility, adopting her as his own daughter.

What do you learn about Mordecai and Esther from these short verses? The family bond between Mordecai and Esther brings out in them many good qualities, including a sense of loyalty and caring in

Mordecai that goes beyond an obligation of duty to his cousin. We see that the bond between them is strong and will prove crucial to the outworking of the story.

Reflect on modern family life. We've come a long way since the 'typical' family unit was considered to be mother, father and 2.4 children. In these days of high divorce rates, couples who never marry, and same sex unions, new ways of describing families have emerged, including the term 'blended families', consisting of a couple, the children they've had together and their children from previous relationships.

## Prayer

Thank you, Father, for family life, all its ups and downs, and for the support and encouragement it can provide in everyday life. Help me always to keep you at the heart of my family.

# Esther's beauty

We now learn that Esther is one of the many girls taken to the palace during the king's search for a new queen. We are not told any details about her former life, apart from the death of her parents and her adoption by Mordecai. Nor are we told what Esther thinks about her enforced removal to the harem, which neither she nor Mordecai could prevent happening.

*Read Chapter 2:8, 9.*

Beauty, we are proverbially told, is only skin deep. King Xerxes may have had youth and beauty as his principal criteria when choosing a new queen, but there is something very special about Esther's beauty and presence. She finds favour with everyone who meets her, including Hegai, the king's eunuch, who gives her special treatment and the best place in the harem. Esther has beauty in her soul.

How far do you think the world judges people by their outward appearance, whether someone is 'easy on the eye', attractive and slim? Is it only among the younger generations that peer pressure exists to wear the right 'labels' or carry the latest smartphone? The Bible speaks about a woman's true beauty lying not in outward appearance – fine clothes and gold jewellery, but in the 'inner self with the lasting beauty of a gentle and quiet spirit, which is very precious in God's sight' (1 Peter 3:3, 4).

## Prayer

Dear Lord, I thank you that you look at the heart, not at outward appearance. May your beauty be reflected in my life.

# Queen Esther

Mordecai continues to watch over and advise Esther from a distance. She is obedient to him when he forbids her to disclose her Jewishness. This is a wise move, as we will see later in the story, and is important for the plot.

*Read Chapter 2:10-18.*

After a whole year of 'beauty treatments', imagine Esther's fear and trepidation when she is finally presented to King Xerxes. She wins his heart, is chosen to succeed Vashti and the lavish celebrations begin. However, even as queen, Esther has few rights and little access to the king. She continues to live in the harem and may have more influence, freedom and authority than the concubines, but her life is very restricted, and she is only allowed to see the king when he summons her.

Even though the name of God has not been mentioned, do you begin to detect the power at work in the shadows, using Esther's natural beauty and loveliness to elevate her to the position of queen, well ahead of any danger that might threaten her and her people? God is always at work in the lives of individuals and nations, totally in control, working out his purposes, even if we can't see it at the time, even if the world seems to be in the grip of evil powers. Can you look back at times in your life when God has been at work, but you haven't realised it until later? Do you believe that God has everything in hand?

## Prayer
Thank you, Lord, for you are almighty and in control of every situation in life that I face, even if it's not apparent at the time. No one and nothing is beyond your love and care. Help me to remember this and put my trust and faith in you.

# 9

# Mordecai uncovers a plot

Esther now temporarily takes a back seat as Mordecai moves centre stage. We reach a key point in the story, one that is crucial to the plot.

*Read Chapter 2:19-23.*

We read that Mordecai has a vantage point, sitting at the king's gate, which indicates his high position as a government official. By chance, he overhears a conspiracy by two of the king's guards to assassinate the king. Mordecai informs Esther, who then tells the king, and the conspirators receive their due punishment. Important for the plot is the official recording of these events. While it is usual for the king to reward acts of loyalty, for some reason this doesn't happen at the time.

Esther continues to be obedient to Mordecai and carries out his wishes. Mordecai is principled, obedient, faithful and loyal to the king and works within the Persian law, without compromising his integrity. One theme of Esther is how the people of God cope with being scattered yet retain their faith in God. There are no prophets to tell them God's word and no priests to intercede for them.

Think about Christians today who live in countries where the government is not favourable to Christianity. How do they live in such a regime without compromising their faith and obedience to God? What price may some Christians have to pay to remain faithful witnesses to God? Have you ever been in a similar situation?

## Prayer

Almighty God, I pray for all those who feel pressured to compromise their faithfulness and obedience to you. Help them to stay strong and persevere.

# Danger – a threat to the Jews

Having met the 'good' characters in the story, Esther and Mordecai, we are now introduced to Haman, their antithesis and the villain of the piece.

*Read Chapter 3:1-6.*

Four years have gone by since Esther became queen. We aren't told why the king chooses to promote Haman to second in command in the Empire, placing complete trust in him. Haman is depicted as arrogant, ambitious and self-serving. He loves the power and authority he wields and measures his own worth by the influence he has over others. Puffed up with pride and self-importance, Haman expects everyone to bow down to him, as the king has commanded. When Mordecai courageously refuses, and Haman becomes aware of his Jewishness, Haman can't contain his anger against Mordecai and his race, and he vows to kill all the Jews in the Persian Empire, which would have included the land of Israel.

Such animosity may appear extreme, but Haman is described as 'the Agagite', an Amalekite. The ongoing conflict between Israel and the Amalekites began during the Exodus and carried on throughout Israel's history. This long-standing mutual hatred would explain why Mordecai is prepared to bow down in homage to the king but not to Haman, and Haman's determination to destroy all the Jews.

Where do evil forces appear to have the upper hand in our present world? We shouldn't become simplistic about the nature of good and evil, nor imagine they are equally balanced forces. The power of evil, though great and never to be underestimated, is miniscule by comparison with our almighty God, who reigns supreme and in total control.

## Prayer

All-powerful God, give me the courage to take a stand wherever I see evil in the world and do what I can, in my small way, to overcome it. Strengthen and protect me with your spiritual armour, I pray.

# Haman puts his plan in place

The focus of the story shifts temporarily from Esther and Mordecai to Haman, who wastes no time in deceiving King Xerxes and persuading him to issue a decree that seals the death warrant for the Jews.

*Read Chapter 3:7-15.*

Acting superstitiously, lots are cast (the *pur* – from which the feast instigated later in the story derives its name) to pick the best time to carry out the murderous plan. Interestingly, the month Haman starts plotting to destroy the Jews is the same month as the Jewish celebration of the Passover, when Jews remembered their deliverance from Egypt (see Exodus 12:1-11). The date is chosen to annihilate all the Jews in the Empire and plunder their goods and is nearly a year off (7 March 473BC). The decree also calls for the same level of destruction that was earlier decreed against the Amalekites (see 1 Samuel 15:3).

Haman bends the truth by not naming the Jews explicitly, falsely accusing this 'certain people' of disobedience to the king and promising a vast sum of money to the king (from plundered wealth) if he backs the plan. In truth, the Jews have their own customs and laws, but they aren't in rebellion against the king, whose weakness is underlined when he gives Haman carte blanche to enforce any law he chooses in the king's name. Xerxes sanctions genocide, unaware that Haman's measures against the Jews will apply to Queen Esther too, and the pair sit down to drink together.

We see Haman given the power and authority to carry out his vindictive plan. If he had succeeded, all God's chosen people would have been wiped out and Jesus would never have been born. It was as serious as that. However, God is at work to undermine this evil plan.

Throughout history, we see racial bigotry, hatred and intolerance, often targeting the Jews. Focus on areas of today's world where racial minorities are currently being persecuted and are suffering.

## Prayer
Make me aware, Lord, of injustice and racial hatred and help me to do what I can to combat these evils in the world.

# Crisis time for the Jewish race

Mordecai and his fellow Jews throughout the Empire hear about Haman's decree and begin to mourn.

*Read Chapter 4:1-3.*

We read of the Jews' reaction to the news: a very public display of fasting, crying and wailing, tearing clothes and putting on sackcloth and ashes. The fasting contrasts markedly with the great feasts and banquets described in previous chapters. Prayer and calling out to God are not mentioned specifically but would have been included. Mordecai turns to God in this time of great danger for his people.

Where do you turn in a crisis? Is God your first or last resort? In times of trouble, are you able to trust God's promises? Although there is no promise of exemption *from* the storms of life, we are given divine protection *in* the storms. Looking back at previous difficulties and seeing how God helped you through them, can give you a better perspective on any present problems, and encourage you to keep going. Remember that nothing can ever separate you from the love of God (Romans 8:38, 39) and even if all else fails, the love of God will remain, like an umbilical cord connecting you to him.

## Prayer

Loving God, in times of trouble may I turn to you. You are my place of refuge and a very present help, only ever a breath away. Not a single sparrow falls to the ground without you knowing. I am more valuable to you than many sparrows and I rejoice at the depth of your love for me.

# Mordecai asks for Esther's help

Isolated in the harem, Esther hears second-hand about Mordecai's behaviour. Highly concerned, she sends one of the king's eunuchs to find out the cause of his distress.

*Read Chapter 4:4-11.*

In this roundabout way, Esther learns of the plot against her people. Mordecai pleads with Esther to go to the king and ask him for mercy for the Jews. She may be the queen and in a favoured position, but Esther knows that even she would risk death if she went to the king without being summoned. Obedient as she is to her cousin, this time she can't possibly do what Mordecai asks.

Who can blame Esther for her initial reluctance and fearfulness? She is thinking about her own safety and security and not considering the bigger picture. Perhaps she thought herself safe in the palace?

The Old Testament shows us that Esther is in good company. There's a long list of people God chooses to do his will but who are reluctant and fearful. Think of Moses, for instance, bargaining with God (Exodus Chapter 3). These are 'ordinary' people made great by God, who resources them for the task in hand and moulds them into people he can work with to carry out his will.

Can you pinpoint times when you have felt God asking you to say or do something and you have been fearful and reluctant? Did you remain silent or were you able to overcome your initial fears? We value our security, even though the security of this world is not guaranteed. What or who do you place your faith and trust in? God is our ultimate security and our safety rests with him.

## Prayer

Lord God, you are my ultimate security and safety. May I look to you and your kingdom and not place my trust in the shifting sands of this world.

# Mordecai won't take no for an answer

Continuing to use messengers to convey their words and feelings, Esther and Mordecai communicate with each other further.

*Read Chapter 4:12-14.*

Mordecai puts Esther under great pressure by insisting she helps her people and tells her some home truths: as a Jew she won't be safe from the decree, even in the palace. Unless Esther acts, she and her family will not survive. Mordecai's faith in God's sovereignty and protection leads him to assume that if Esther won't help, another way of saving the Jewish people will be found. God's power and resources are not limited by human unwillingness. Mordecai tells Esther it's her destiny to help her people, it's why she has been made queen. God has been overseeing events, putting her in the right place at the right time.

Esther is one of several Old Testament characters chosen and used by God in a position of authority in a pagan society. We read that Daniel, who was deported to Babylon, didn't compromise his principles. Parallels can also be drawn between Esther and the story of Joseph, where the action takes place in a foreign court, and the hero is given authority and the way to save his people.

Do you believe that God has a purpose for the situations he puts you in? Is it apparent at the time or only on looking back? Have you ever felt 'drawn' to a person or place 'at the right moment'? Did it seem to be rather more than pure chance or coincidence?

## Prayer

Sovereign Lord, help me to recognise your purpose for me in the small, everyday things of life. Give me eyes to see and ears to hear and help me to be obedient.

## 15

# Esther rises to the challenge

Persuaded by Mordecai's reasoning, Esther agrees to help her people.

*Read Chapter 4:15-17.*

In preparation for going to the king to plead the cause of her people, Esther begins to take the initiative and tells Mordecai to organise a three-day fast, which would presumably have included prayer, although it isn't mentioned here. A key verse is her statement: 'If I die, I die.' We see the courage shown by Mordecai and Esther, who both acted, and God was able to use them to save his people. But how much of a hero is Esther and to what extent is she driven by self-interest? She acts reluctantly and only risks her life when pressured by Mordecai, and on realising she is also in danger. How much choice and free will does Esther have to say no? Is the fatalism in her words justifiable, as she rises to the challenge in a seemingly hopeless situation?

Can you put yourself in Esther's shoes as she prepares to go to the king and plead for the Jews? Have you ever faced what looks like a hopeless situation? How did you deal with it? Esther looks for support from the other Jews at this difficult time, calling on them to fast. When you are facing challenges, do you have fellow Christians to turn to? Do you share your problems with them and draw strength from the faith and fellowship of others? Can you rely on them to pray for you and support you in other ways, too?

## Prayer

Lord God of hope, even in the darkest moments, help me to trust in your care and protection. Thank you for the people you send who are willing to walk alongside me at such times.

# Esther goes to the king

Try to picture Esther's fear and trepidation as the day arrives and she prepares to go to the king.

*Read Chapter 5:1-8.*

Esther's fears prove groundless: the king is pleased to see her and welcomes her request. How much have fasting and prayer influenced the king's favourable response? Esther does her duty but needs God's protection and wisdom to help her. We begin to see Esther's strength of character emerging in her conversation with the king. She is quick-witted, determined, clever and resourceful in her planning and willing to risk her life to save her people.

Self-sacrifice and acting for the good of others runs counter to the world's outlook, which tells us to focus primarily on our own interests, to look after 'number one'. In March 2018, a French gendarme, Lieutenant-Colonel Arnaud Beltrame, made the news headlines around the world. He died from gunshot wounds when he took the place of a female cashier being held hostage by a radical Islamist in a supermarket siege in southern France, knowing that the terrorist had already killed three people, and he would probably die too. It has emerged that this man was a devout Catholic, taking quite literally Christ's teaching to be willing to lay down his life for others and follow his example. His exceptional courage and selflessness has led to comparisons being made with others before him, such as Saint Maximilian Kolbe, a Polish Franciscan priest who volunteered to be executed in Auschwitz in 1941, in the place of a family man.

## Prayer

Lord, it's highly unlikely that such a great act of self-sacrifice will ever be asked of me, but you call me to be faithful in small ways, so that I can be trusted with bigger things. Let it be so, with your help, I pray.

# 17

# Haman's rage against Mordecai intensifies

Advised by his wife and friends, Haman takes drastic measures to rid himself of Mordecai, once and for all.

*Read Chapter 5:9-14.*

Haman's pride, boasting and self-glorification are in complete contrast to the actions of Mordecai and Esther. Haman hates Mordecai because of his refusal to bow down and pay homage to him, but principally because of his Jewishness.

The Jews were a racial minority in Persia and Haman's plot to exterminate them all, beginning with Mordecai, has strong links with the intentions of the Nazi regime. Indeed, the term genocide to describe the destruction of a race was first used in 1943. In more recent times we have seen the persecution of minorities, terror campaigns, attempts at ethnic cleansing and the annihilation of whole races in

Rwanda and Bosnia. Lately, the eyes of the world have been upon Myanmar (formerly Burma) where the Rohingya Muslims, a large minority ethnic group classed as immigrants, have been denied their basic human rights. It's been a textbook example of ethnic cleansing, with hundreds of refugees reportedly killed and many more displaced.

The Bible is clear that God makes no distinctions based on race (see Galatians 3:28). God made all people in his own image, so every person on earth, regardless of race, has intrinsic worth and we are called to respect and accord everyone their God-given dignity as a human being. The measure of our humanity is indicated in the way we treat our neighbour, whether known to us or in some distant country. How can we, as Christians, counteract racial hatred in our world today?

## Prayer

I may seem a very small cog in the world's eyes, Lord, but let me play my part in the fight against racism. Saying or doing nothing isn't an option.

# 18

# A happy coincidence

When it appears that things couldn't be much worse for Mordecai, we reach a turning point in the story.

*Read Chapter 6:1-3.*

At an opportune time, the king suffers from insomnia, reads about Mordecai's earlier faithfulness and learns he received no reward for his actions in exposing the assassination plot. The name of God may not have been mentioned in this story, but divine intervention in events is clear. In the ancient world, sleeplessness would be regarded as being sent by God. God is at work, controlling and directing all these 'coincidences'.

The recollection of an incident that occurred earlier and had been forgotten may *seem* coincidental, but we understand that God's hand is on the situation, bringing about the fulfilment of his purposes for his people. Are you able to look back on your life and see similar coincidences, sometimes referred to by

Christians as 'God-instances'? Do you find yourself wondering why God chooses to act in this way? The Bible teaches that events can come together for good (see Romans 8:28). Are you able to accept and trust how God works in your life?

## Prayer

Sovereign Lord, teach me to recognise the times when I have experienced God-instances, not merely chance or coincidence. Help me to put my faith in your ways and to be thankful for your hand upon my life.

# 19

# Delicious irony

Haman arrives at the palace to ask for permission to hang Mordecai. In a series of misunderstandings worthy of any good farce, Haman's plans begin to unravel.

*Read Chapter 6:4-11.*

Blinded by self-aggrandisement, Haman automatically believes that he is the one the king wants to honour. Imagine how crestfallen he feels at being ordered by the king to honour Mordecai instead of hanging him. Through gritted teeth he leads Mordecai along the streets. We are left to wonder how Mordecai reacted: was he baffled and confused? Did he recognise God's hand at work, his exquisite, perfect timing and give thanks? In true pantomime fashion, we see the villain of the story begin to get his comeuppance and events move towards a happy ending. However, there are still many obstacles for our heroes to overcome.

God acts in his way and in his timing. We need to be patient and submit to his authority. We may not know what lies ahead, but by staying close to God, who is able to see every detail of our future, whose purposes are loving and who promises to provide everything that we need to face that future, we can go forward with a new sense of freedom.

Do you believe that God has everything in hand? In the pressures and demands of everyday life, are you patient enough to wait for God's timings? Can you trust him?

## Prayer

Lord God, evil may have its day in our world and appear to have the upper hand, but eventually evil forces are always overcome and punished. Help me to remember this and wait patiently for you to act.

# 20

# Haman's decline and fall

How suddenly Haman's fortunes turn; his earlier happiness and high spirits now give way to grief.

*Read Chapter 6:12-14.*

Haman's wife and advisers have enough insight to recognise that Haman can't win against Mordecai, because of his Jewishness – implying the power of God – and predict his downfall. Haman is no longer directing affairs and is taken off by the king's advisers to Esther's banquet.

We have seen the escalation of evil in Haman, consumed as he is by his hatred of the Jews. Now his downfall begins to look inevitable, for such hatred must surely be punished, and the threatened Jewish holocaust avoided. Do you find yourself wondering why it often takes so long to overcome evil? Is it always a case of waiting for God to act, trusting in his timing or does evil sometimes prosper because *we* don't act soon enough?

Throughout history, Jews have been persecuted because they are a minority and different. Regimes like the Third Reich played on people's fears and used the Jews as a scapegoat to blame for Germany's economic problems. Anti-Semitism, a warning sign of serious problems within a society, is currently high on the political agenda. Hatred may begin with anti-Semitism, but it can escalate to include other minorities, as we saw with the Nazi atrocities.

Why did six million Jews have to die in the holocaust? How could a God of love and compassion allow the mass extermination of his chosen people? Could their suffering have been cut short and what more could the Christian Church have done? Evil can prosper when good people do nothing to stop it. What can we learn from the Christians who did resist and did all they could to put a stop to evil?

## Prayer

Almighty God, we need to learn the lessons of history and play our part in current world events. It's not enough to look at atrocities from the past, feel guilty and simply say, 'Never again.'

# 21

# Esther makes her request

After a short absence, Esther takes centre stage again. The seventh banquet of the story moves the plot along, as Esther reveals the plight of her people.

*Read Chapter 7:1-10.*

Haman had been economical with the truth and kept from Xerxes the identity of the 'certain people' (3:8). Picture Haman's reaction as Esther courageously pleads for herself and her people and reveals who is behind the plot. The irony piles up as Haman, who had been furious when Mordecai wouldn't bow down to him, now falls before Esther and begs her for his life. The king returns, witnesses the scene and misinterprets it as attempted rape. Haman's fate is sealed, and the final irony is when he is hanged on the same gallows that he had built for Mordecai.

We see the steady rise of good and the defeat of evil. The Bible is vocal on comeuppance – see, for example, Proverbs 26:27, Daniel 6:24 and Psalm 7:15, 16.

Reflect on Christ's suffering and death on the cross, as he took upon himself the sins of all humanity. Look beyond the physical and mental suffering he endured to the power of the cross, the victory won, the loud cry of triumph: 'It is finished' (John 19:30). As Christians we can trust that evil has already been defeated by the death and resurrection of Jesus and he will return at the end of time to bring in the eternal kingdom of God. How do you live in the light of this promise?

## Prayer

In the new heaven and the new earth at the end of time, evil, death, sickness, sorrow and suffering will be no more. Loving Lord, help me to hold onto this hope of a perfect eternity to come.

# 22

# The 'good' are rewarded

In a complete role reversal, Esther receives Haman's entire estate and Mordecai is appointed to oversee it.

*Read Chapter 8:1, 2.*

When Esther reveals the nature of her relationship with Mordecai, Xerxes presents Mordecai with the signet ring that had belonged to Haman. We have the happy ending for our heroes, who were willing to give up everything in their fight against evil. Their good deeds are rewarded by Xerxes with great material wealth, which is the only way he understands. Were Esther and Mordecai expecting such a reward?

In the Old Testament people believed that material blessings (including large families, abundant crops, herds and flocks, and victory in battle) would be theirs if they were faithful to God's covenants and laws, so it was assumed the rich had been well blessed by God. Consider the modern-day Prosperity Gospel, which promotes the idea that Christians should expect the same kind of material blessings enjoyed by God's people in the Old Testament. Financial blessing is the will of God for Christians, if they are faithful, this gospel says, and suffering can be bypassed. In your experience, is this theology played out in today's world? Does it have validity? How does it sit with New Testament teaching, especially Jesus' Sermon on the Mount?

## Prayer

Teach me, good Lord,
to serve you as you deserve,
to give and not to count the cost,
to fight and not to heed the wounds,
to toil and not to seek for rest,
to labour and not to ask for any reward,
save that of knowing that I do your will.
Amen.

*(Saint Ignatius of Loyola)*

# 23

# Not yet out of the woods

Esther and Mordecai may be safe, but the Jewish nation is still in peril.

*Read Chapter 8:3-6.*

Haman's decree hangs over the Jewish people. Driven by her selfless concern and not content with personal safety alone, Esther courageously makes a plea for her people, a new decree to overrule the existing one.

Many courageous men and women throughout history are remembered for their selflessness and concern with the greater good, risking their own safety to promote a cause, for example, those who resisted the Nazi regime. German Lutheran Pastor Dietrich Bonhoeffer was arrested in 1943 for his part in the German Resistance Movement and was executed two years later. In 1955 in the USA, African-American Rosa Parks put herself in a dangerous situation when she refused to give up her seat on a bus and move to the back. The symbolism of defying the established law of the South and the resulting publicity led to a greater awareness of the problem. Her act is credited with being one of the major sparks of the American civil rights movement and she is remembered worldwide for her quiet strength and her resolve to do what was right. Some years later, in 1963, Martin Luther King Jr's 'I have a dream' speech boldly denounced the racism that was so ingrained in the USA at the time. What can we learn from such people?

## Prayer

Heavenly Father, as I look to the selflessness, concern and compassion for others that many well-known figures in history have displayed, I thank you for their fine example and remember the supreme self-sacrifice of Jesus, who gave up his life for me.

# 24

# A dilemma solved

The problem remains that Haman's decree is irrevocable. Granted the king's seal of approval, it can't be reversed, not even by the king himself.

*Read Chapter 8:7-14.*

Given total freedom by King Xerxes, Esther and Mordecai write a new decree on behalf of the Jews and seal it with the king's signet ring. This new decree can't formally revoke the original but will counter it, giving the Jews the right to assemble and protect themselves against attack, allowing them to destroy, kill and annihilate, and plunder their enemies' property. It comes two months and ten days after the proclamation of Haman's edict and is to be carried out on one specific day: the same day decreed by Haman for the extermination of the Jews. Permission is therefore given for self-defence against genocide and the wording of 8:9-13 echoes 3:12-14.

We see the cleverness of Esther and Mordecai in finding a solution to their people's dilemma, guided by God in the shadows. God is working out his purpose through their faithfulness and devotion to their people. When we make ourselves available, God can use us in his service. What can you learn from Esther's story about how people are called by God? In the Temple, the prophet Isaiah heard God asking, 'Whom shall I send, and who will go for us?' He responded wholeheartedly, 'Here am I; send me!' (See Isaiah 6:8.)

## Prayer

Here I am, wholly available; use me, holy Lord. Give me the courage to respond to your call and serve you faithfully in the everyday things of life.

## 25

# Celebrations in Susa –
# let joy be unconfined

After the sackcloth and ashes, and all the fasting, weeping and mourning, at last there comes a time for the Jews to feast and celebrate. Sorrow is turned to joy.

*Read Chapter 8:15-17.*

It's a personal triumph for Mordecai and a time of joy and gladness for all the Jewish people. They are now honoured, feared and revered, so much so that many people of other nationalities become Jews themselves. Throughout the Empire there is feasting and celebration. Mordecai, while faithful in his service to the king, had been willing to risk his life for his people and he has received praise, honour and wealth. The Jews are guaranteed protection throughout the Empire, religious freedom and privileges.

We are promised that God will turn situations around. Have you experienced this in your life? How do you respond on occasions when you recognise beyond doubt that God's hand is on your life and that he cares about whatever concerns you – the big and small things alike? God deserves our heartfelt praise and worship, imperfect and inadequate though this may be.

'You have turned my mourning into dancing; you have taken off my sackcloth and clothed me with joy, so that my soul may praise you and not be silent. O Lord my God, I will give thanks to you for ever' (Psalm 30:11, 12).

## Prayer

Psalm 30, verse 5 says that 'Weeping may linger for the night, but joy comes with the morning.' Loving God, give me patience to wait for you in the darkness of night and trust that the morning will come.

# The triumph of the Jews

As in all the best stories, good finally overcomes evil and there is a happy ending.

*Read Chapter 9:1-4.*

Haman's decree had given the right for anyone to kill the Jews on a certain day (the thirteenth day of the twelfth month) and take their property. His decree couldn't be cancelled but the new law now gives the Jews the right to fight back and defend themselves. In a complete reversal, the Jews triumph over all those who are opposed to them. No one can withstand them, and they have the backing of the king's forces. Mordecai's prestige and power increase but they are used for the good of the people, in direct contrast with the self-serving Haman.

Do you watch the TV news bulletins and feel that it's just one awful story after another? It's so easy to adopt a negative, pessimistic mindset and conclude that things will never change. In May 2017, at the Manchester Arena, 23 people were killed and 120 injured in an Islamist terror attack. One year on, hundreds of people came together in the city to remember the victims. The atmosphere was positive, a city united in love and solidarity, determined not to be beaten by terrorism. Surely these are the news stories to focus on, where people are convinced that good can come from bad and refuse to be overwhelmed by evil? If we stand firm, good will ultimately triumph over evil in our world. We wait for God's timings and ask for his patience.

## Prayer

Lord God of hope, I'm in danger of feeling swamped by constant bad news stories. Help me to believe that good can come from bad and that by working together, we can overcome the evil in this world.

# 27

# **Great bloodshed**

So, a happy ending for the Jews as they defend themselves and kill their enemies.

*Read Chapter 9:5-16.*

Acting to protect themselves against those who wanted to annihilate them, the Jews kill many thousands, but they do not take any plunder, even though they have been given permission to do so. You may have mixed feelings at this point, when reading about the wholesale slaughter of the Jews' enemies. Does the story sound unnecessarily bloodthirsty, as Esther asks for the ten sons of Haman to be hanged? After the permitted two days, the killings end, and it can be argued that this was limited action carried out in self-defence. Vengeance, retribution and selfish gain were not the primary goals.

How do you respond to this story? The Jewish people fought violence with violence, an eye for an eye, kill or be killed. Can we make allowances for their behaviour because they lived in brutal, less-enlightened times? What about the violence in our world today? The nature of God has not changed since the days of Esther, for he remains the God of justice who will not tolerate sin and evil. Do you think there is a contradiction between Old and New Testament teaching on the permissibility of violence and the treatment of our enemies? How do you make sense of seemingly incompatible teachings?

## Prayer

Almighty God, it's been said that an eye for an eye makes the whole world blind. Help me to understand this difficult theme of violence in the Bible. Grant me a better insight into your nature, especially your justice and mercy.

# 28

# The Feast of Purim is established

As part of the joy and celebrations, a great feast is established, one that is still celebrated by Jews every year.

*Read Chapter 9:17-32.*

To keep the memory of the events surrounding the triumph of the Jews alive, they are recorded by Mordecai and he calls for an annual celebration of their deliverance, including giving presents of food to one another and gifts to the poor. The name of the feast derives from earlier in the story (3:7), when Haman cast lots (the *pur*) to determine when his plot to destroy the Jews would take place. The feast is a reminder that, by the grace of God, the Jewish nation will survive, even in the face of great danger and the threat of annihilation.

Nowadays, the Feast of Purim is celebrated by Jews as a symbol of God's deliverance. Regarded as a time for charitable deeds, with much dressing up, carnivals and partying, it's a secular rather than a spiritual festival, with no religious ceremony. Traditionally, the most important custom is the reading of the Purim story from the scroll of Esther, with Jews usually attending the synagogue for this special reading and booing loudly whenever Haman's name is mentioned!

The original meaning of Purim may be lost amidst all the celebrations and it's more an excuse for partying and having a good time. Also lost on many people is the real reason for the special times, like Christmas and Easter, when Christians celebrate God's specific acts and his goodness. How do you help to preserve the original meaning of these times?

## Prayer

Lord God, help me not to compromise my faith and be ready to tell and show the people I meet what Easter and Christmas mean to me.

# 29

# The epilogue

The short, final chapter is a summary of Mordecai's greatness.

*Read Chapter 10:1-3.*

Esther, apparently, has disappeared from the scene – the last we read of her is in the previous chapter. It's unclear what happened to her. Did she die as queen or did she fall out of favour? Esther may have the honour of being one of only two women in the entire Bible with a book named after her, but it often looks as though Mordecai is the real star of the story. He is held in high regard by fellow Jews because he uses his power and influence for good and doesn't turn his back on those in need. However, Esther's legacy lives on in the book that bears her name and in the annual Purim celebrations. Details of her inner beauty, courage, compassion, kindness and good nature are there for all to read.

With Haman we saw corruption and the abuse of authority, but with Mordecai, now second only to King Xerxes in power and authority in the kingdom, God is able to use him for the benefit of his people. You may not think that you have much power and influence in local or national affairs, but how can you use what you do have to help those in need?

## Prayer

Lord, may I use the power and influence I have for the good of others. It may not seem much but let me do what I can.

# 30

# Summing up

The Book of Esther is a great deal more than an entertaining story of good versus evil that has lasting significance for the Jewish nation. It contains so much that is relevant to today's world and the Christian daily walk with God. We like to believe that we live in more enlightened times but to what extent has basic human nature changed since Old Testament days? We don't need to look far in our world to see inequality, oppression, discrimination, hatred, intolerance, racial bigotry, genocide, ethnic cleansing, violence and bloodshed.

Haman is the personification of evil, illustrating what happens when someone is totally consumed and blinded by hatred. Yet every person is capable of evil, with the free will to commit sin and disobey God. Evil doesn't always appear evil, deceiving, deluding and seducing people into believing that moral limits and boundaries shouldn't be there, so they are free to cross them, and the subsequent reward will be wisdom, knowledge, power and happiness.

God is in control of history, as the Book of Esther shows, and is working in our lives, whether we perceive him or not. He promises to save us from the evil in this world and deliver us from sin and death. The Book of Revelation tells us that Jesus will return to this earth and finish what he began at the cross and resurrection. At the end of time, after the final battle between the cosmic forces of good and evil, the power of evil will finally be destroyed and there will be peace and justice over all the world: a new heaven and a new earth.

*Read Revelation 21:1-4.*

What has the Book of Esther taught you? How have these devotions spurred you on in your daily walk with God?

## Prayer

Heavenly Father, help me to remember the story of Esther and its relevance to life today. But above all, let me never overlook the sacrifice of Jesus, and his victory over sin and death.

# Also available

## Deep Calls to Deep
### 1501578

In this inspiring meditative collection,
Linda Ottewell has chosen an extract from a Psalm
as a springboard for her thoughts and ideas,
which are presented as a short reflection and
then rounded off with a prayer or poem, a verse or
two from Scripture, or part of a well-loved hymn.

**www.kevinmayhew.com**